Beside Still *Waters*

40 Daily Devotionals Written from the
Heart During the 2020 Pandemic

Jennifer Ramsey

WestBow Press books may be ordered through booksellers or by contacting:

WestBow Press
A Division of Thomas Nelson & Zondervan
1663 Liberty Drive
Bloomington, IN 47403
www.westbowpress.com
844-714-3454

ISBN: 978-1-6642-3896-1 (sc)
ISBN: 978-1-6642-3897-8 (e)

Library of Congress Control Number: 2021913298

Print information available on the last page.

WestBow Press rev. date: 08/23/2021

WESTBOW
PRESS®
A DIVISION OF THOMAS NELSON
& ZONDERVAN

Dedication

Thank you, Jesus, for first loving me.

To God be the glory.

"To God our Savior, who alone is wise, be glory and majesty, dominion and power, both now and forever. Amen." Jude 25 (NKJV)

Preface

Psalm 23:1-2 (ESV)

The LORD is my shepherd; I shall not want.
He makes me lie down in green pastures.
He leads me beside still waters.

As I consider the year this book represents, I want to give you a framework in which you may understand its origin. As a registered nurse of almost 20 years, the year of 2020 posed a great challenge for me and many health care providers. Amidst the everyday changes, new procedures, and care guidelines, it challenged and changed our ability to provide care to individuals the way in which we were accustomed. Bedside care turned into phone care. Care discussions with fellow health care providers, once done easily and frequently face to face, began to take place periodically over remote video conferencing and through confidential online discussions. Most of these writings, in their original form, were daily emails to co-workers in the health clinic where I work and provide care to university students. During the time when our work desks were in our individual homes, and each of us experienced hurt and chaos in different ways during the pandemic, those daily emails served as a way for me to connect, encourage, and turn our team's focus to the One who does not change. This enabled us to be comforted and strengthened by His Word. Through the encouragement of my co-workers, friends, and family, those emails are compiled into the devotional format that you hold in your hands. I hope and pray that they bring comfort to your heart, and that as you face challenges in this life, you will remember He is your shepherd and will lead you beside still waters. I'd also encourage you to meditate on the Scripture I've referenced and dig deeper in your own personal Bible study.

Thank you for the privilege of allowing me to be a small part of your journey.

By His gentle mercy and amazing grace, He is my Good Shepherd,

Jennifer

Contents

Come to Me

Matthew 11:28-30 (NKJV)
"Come to me, all who labor and are heavy laden, and I will give you rest.
Take my yoke upon you, and learn from me, for I am gentle and lowly in heart, and
you will find rest for your souls. For my yoke is easy, and my burden is light."

"Come to me." It is a simple command, yet at times it's the last place we go when we are tired and burdened by the world.

My brother was recently diagnosed with COVID-19 and is recovering in the ICU. In addition to the local and national unrest we are experiencing, this was yet another blow to my weary soul.

The song "Rest for Your Soul" by Austin French has been a balm for my spirit, especially these lyrics: "There's One who knows the heavy you hold."

Praise God! He not only knows each of us and our circumstances, He walks with us through them. His load is light, and we can rest in Him when we lay our burdens at His feet. I don't know what your heavy burden is, but He does, and all He says is "come."

My dad, months before he went to be with Jesus, wrote today's Scripture in a letter to me as an encouragement to find my rest in Him in difficult times, reminding me that our Lord Jesus gave us this promise. What a precious gift Jesus offers when we come to Him, and how blessed we are that He always keeps His promises.

He is gentle, He is gracious, and He is good. He offers us rest and peace that surpasses all understanding.

Let Him carry you.

Is It Well with Your Soul?

Psalm 94:19 (ESV)
"When the cares of my heart are many,
Your consolations cheer my soul."

God has a way of bringing us comfort when we are burdened by the cares of this world. Sometimes He graciously gives us this comfort through His Word, His Spirit, or His people. I am often reminded of old hymns that are a soothing salve on my soul during difficult times.

The saints of old used their walk with the Lord, perseverance in trials, and steadfast focus on The Lord to shed light on the turmoil they faced. From their words and shared hope, we, too, can receive the comfort of our Savior.

One such hymn is "It is Well with My Soul," written by Horatio Spafford after losing 4 daughters at sea. This is a tragedy I find hard to grasp due to its incredible weight, and yet I find the magnitude of God's grace to be greater still through Spafford's words. Listen to his words as he writes amidst his pain: "When peace like a river attendeth my way / when sorrows like sea billows roll / whatever my lot, Thou hast taught me to say / it is well with my soul."

During times of difficulty and heaviness of heart, verse 2 of this hymn stands out in bold print "Though trials should come / let this blest assurance control / that Christ has regarded my helpless estate / and hath shed His own blood for my soul!"

Oh, how His consolations cheer my soul!

Strength Renewed

Isaiah 40:28-31 (NKJV)
"Have you not known?
Have you not heard?
The everlasting God, the Lord,
The Creator of the ends of the earth,
Neither faints nor is weary.
His understanding is unsearchable.
He gives power to the weak,
And to those who have no might He increases strength.
Even the youths shall faint and be weary,
And the young men shall utterly fall,
But those who wait on the Lord
Shall renew their strength.
They shall mount up with wings like eagles,
They shall run and not be weary,
They shall walk and not faint."

I often catch myself thinking about waiting. Who doesn't find themselves waiting for something or in need of strength, especially in these uncertain times? Consider Webster's definition of waiting: "to stay in place, in expectation of." What are you waiting for? Do you need strength?

Many things these days have induced waiting for me, probably like most of you. I'm waiting for:
- the stay-at-home order to lift
- for businesses to return to usual
- for the waves of change and government orders to cease for the peak of COVID-19 to hit the United States (in which I am bracing internally for impact)
- for the numbers of cases of the virus to decrease
- for a vaccine

- for a definite treatment
- for masks to be made
- for ventilators to be produced
- the possibility of the virus to hit someone I know
- for the sun to shine
- for "normal" life to return (although after this so many things will be different)

Today, my need for strength came specifically when the stay-at-home orders were prolonged. More waiting. It hit hard, thinking not only of the personal impact, but the larger scale impact, as well. Personally, working from home, homeschooling, and lack of face-to-face relationships brought many challenges. The frustrations and roller coaster emotions of sudden change, along with the grief of watching my family struggle with these things at times seemed overwhelming. Questions of the larger scale impact on the next generation also plagued my mind and brought me to my knees in prayer. I needed a grace sufficient and grace abounding that only the Lord can give.

Maybe the better question to ask ourselves is: "Who are you waiting on?"

This Scripture calls us to wait on the Lord, and He promises to renew our strength. I'm thankful for this reassurance and promise that He isn't weary and understands all things. We can wait on and trust in Him to renew our strength in days such as these.

May He renew your strength as you wait expectantly on Him.

Troubled Waters

Isaiah 43:1-4a (NKJV)
"But now thus says the Lord,
He who created you, O Jacob,
He who formed you, O Israel:
'Fear not, for I have redeemed you;
I have called you by name, you are Mine.
When you pass through the waters, I will be with you;
and through the rivers, they shall not overwhelm you;
when you walk through fire you shall not be burned,
and the flame shall not consume you.
For I am the Lord your God,
the Holy One of Israel, your Savior.
I give Egypt as your ransom,
Cush and Seba in exchange for you.
Because you are precious in my eyes,
and honored, and I love you.'"

"When you pass through …" What a beautiful reminder today that we are not alone and are going to pass through whatever seeks to overwhelm us.

COVID-19 is starting to hit closer to home in our lives now, with a friend's family member in the hospital, a friend caring for first responders' children who are at increased risk of exposure, the numbers in my hometown increasing, and loved ones struggling with the stay-at-home restrictions. These things are heavy on my heart as I consider these effects on each individual and overall well beings.

When praying through today's passage in Isaiah and seeing the dates I've written by it through the years (dating back to 2010), I'm reminded of His faithfulness to me and my family through the years and my heart is comforted. As His children, we are precious in His sight, He loves us, and He has promised to be with us. The God who has conquered sin and death and overcome the world is with those who have trusted Jesus as their Savior.

What a great reminder to turn our eyes from the troubled waters that start to overwhelm us to the One who is with us!

To Him be the glory!

Radiant

Psalm 34:5 (ESV)
"Those who look to him are radiant, and their faces shall never be ashamed."

I was reminded of this Scripture after listening to a sermon titled "Radiant Hope" by Alistair Begg. The word "radiant" stuck out to me, and it reminded me of the film Charlotte's Web, based on the book by E.B. White. In the moment when Charlotte's web spells the word "Radiant," the camera made sure that Wilbur's face shined bright and the web itself glistened in the sunlight. Just as the web glistened as it reflected the sun, and as the moon reflects the sun, we reflect His glory. Not in or of ourselves, but all to Him be the glory.

With that picture in mind, Webster's Dictionary defines radiant as not only "vividly bright" but also "marked by or expressive of love, confidence, or happiness." This definition enriches this Scripture as we are instructed to radiate God's Truth.

Our hope and confidence are found when we look to Jesus, the Author and Finisher of our faith (Hebrews 12:2a). In Him alone can we have complete confidence and joy in times such as these.

May you be radiant today as you look to Him.

Surprised by Joy

John 3: 36a (ESV)
"Whoever believes in the Son has eternal life."

While meditating on this Scripture, I was reminded of Isaiah 55, and how the heading for this passage in the NKJV version is "An Invitation to Abundant Life." Take a moment to read this passage in your Bible.

Life. What is this life Christ offers, especially in the middle of a pandemic, when our lives are turned upside down and far from what we had once enjoyed or even hoped for?

Isaiah describes Christ's invitation to His free gift of life, but this is not something we only get to enjoy in eternity! We can experience His blessings now, and as Isaiah 55:2b (NKJV) states, our "souls can delight in abundance."

C.S. Lewis, a famous theologian, scholar, and author, wrote a book in 1955 titled "Surprised by Joy." When I heard that title, I found myself thinking, "I'd like to be surprised by joy today." How about you? Who wouldn't desire to be surprised by joy today?

As I looked further in this passage, verse 12 says, "For you shall go out with joy." Jesus Himself and the life that He offers bring the fullness of joy. When we believe and walk in that truth, we find that He blesses us with an abundance for our souls and sends us out with joy.

May you be surprised by joy this day.

The Rock

Psalm 18:1-3 (ESV)
"The Lord Is my Rock and my Fortress.
I love you, O Lord, my strength.
The Lord is my Rock and my Fortress and my Deliverer,
my God, my Rock, in whom I take refuge,
my Shield, and the Horn of my salvation, my Stronghold.
I call upon the Lord, who is worthy to be praised,
and I am saved from my enemies."

I write this after my first experience of an earthquake. With my chair shaking underneath me, the thought of the Lord as my Rock seems all the more glorious. We must remember this hope of our sure foundation, even when the earth itself shakes!

In Psalm 18:7, David writes, "Then the earth shook and trembled." We can probably all relate to a time when our lives felt unstable, whether from a pandemic, relationship troubles, or other situations that make our worlds shake and tremble. The picture of the Lord as my Rock and Fortress infuses strength into my weary heart.

Do you sense His stability? Do you see His steadfastness? We can feel His power in an earthquake, but what a glorious truth it is that the same God who makes the earth shake is our Rock, Fortress and Deliverer! He indeed is worthy of our praise.

Lean into The Rock and His unchanging grace today.

Faith Declared

Habakkuk 3:17-19 (NKJV)

"Though the fig tree may not blossom, nor fruit be on the vines; Though the labor of the olive may fail, and the fields yield no food; Though the flock may be cut off from the fold, and there be no herd in the stalls — Yet I will rejoice in the Lord, I will joy in the God of my salvation. The Lord God is my strength; He will make my feet like deer's feet, And He will make me walk on my high hills."

I've always loved this passage in Habakkuk where the prophet is declaring his faith and trust in God despite his circumstances. He is determined to walk by faith, not by sight. He has confidence in the Lord no matter what and rejoices in the midst of it all.

When he was writing this, Habakkuk faced the uncertainty and imminent destruction of his nation, Judah, by Babylon. In verse 16, just before his exuberant faith declaration, he describes the fear that caused his body to tremble.

Can you relate? We will remember where we sat when the global pandemic hit, when stay-at-home orders were placed, when "essential" and "nonessential" became commonplace language, and uncertainty abounded at work, home, in our country, and around the world.

But we, too, can "rejoice in the Lord" and "joy in the God of my salvation." We can declare "the Lord God is my strength" and trust Him to help us walk on our high hills even when the proverbial sheep are scattered and have no fold in which to rest.

What a Mighty God we serve, worthy of praise, honor, and glory! He is our strength and song, a very present help in trouble.

May you, too, rejoice this day in the Lord.

Sweetly Broken

1 Corinthians 11:24 (NKJV)
"And when He had given thanks, He broke the bread and said, "Take, eat. This is My body which is broken for you. Do this in remembrance of Me.""

Maundy Thursday is a beautiful day to prepare our hearts to celebrate our Savior's death and resurrection on Easter weekend. As I listen to the worship song "Sweetly Broken" by Jeremy Riddle, it reminded me some of what Jesus did for us at the cross. Glorious, isn't He?

As I meditate on the title "Sweetly Broken," it helps me understand the sweetness of knowing of the bitter cup that Jesus drank on our behalf, in submission to His Father. It also reminded me of a quote by Oswald Chambers: "If God has made your cup sweet, drink it with grace; or even if He has made it bitter, drink it in communion with Him."

Is your cup bitter these days? Are there things happening in your life that are distressing or unpleasant? It's probably easy to think of hardships during this pandemic, but even after this is over, trials will still come, just in different shapes and sizes. When those times come, drink in sweet communion with our Savior. Live in thankfulness during bitter times, remembering what He has accomplished.

The cup that God has given me has been, at many times, bitter. I've tasted bitter waters: Some of my own choices, some of others, and some out of anyone's control.

Do these bitter waters taste familiar to you?

- defeat
- loss
- fear
- emotional or physical pain
- financial stress

- relational breakdown
- estrangement from loved ones
- depression
- loss of health
- isolation
- job loss
- watching your own children suffer
- loneliness
- divorce
- trauma
- grief

Most of these bitter waters are just part of living in a broken world. These circumstances taste bitter, but for a moment, look at the sweetness that's in the cup because of Him.

Jesus took the bitter cup so gloriously, and by doing so set a divine example for us to follow (Luke 22-24). In Luke 22, Jesus talks to His Father about the cup before Him, referring to the cross. After His prayer in the Garden of Gethsemane, Jesus submits to the Father, stating, "Not my will, but Yours be done" (Luke 22:42 NKJV).

Hebrews 12:2b (NKJV) says, "Who for the joy that was set before Him endured the cross, despising the shame, and has sat down at the right hand of the throne of God." His joy was fulfilling the will of the Father, suffering the penalty of God's wrath for all of our sins so that we may have eternal life with Him. Our sufferings don't compare to what Christ endured for us, but He gives us an example to follow and an encouragement to endure.

Broken for you, broken for me.

May you be sweetly broken and surrendered to whatever cup God has placed in front of you.

In Everything Give Thanks

1 Thessalonians 5:18 (ESV)
"Give thanks in all circumstances; for this is the will of God in Christ Jesus for you."

Day 4 of a new puppy. This little guy has brought my family much joy, laughter, and loss of sleep! I look at his adorable face and snuggle his fluffy hair and am thankful that "God made the beast of the earth according to its kind, cattle according to its kind, and everything that creeps on the earth according to its kind. And God saw that it was good" (Genesis 1:25 NKJV).

How awesome of Creator God to create a small little fluffy companion for us to love and enjoy! What a special blessing for our family he is. Of course, there are challenges to a new puppy: Changes in the routine, crate training, housebreaking, chewing on everything, and nighttime whining and needs. But oh, there are sweet joys! Those first barks, tug of war, curiosity, discovery of grass, little licks, excited runs to you, fearful little paws on frozen grass tips, burrowing nose in your lap, and playful exuberance are worth the sleepless nights and frequent messes.

Joys, challenges, and sorrows are all part of this life. Motherhood is a good example of this. My precious girls are now into teenage years, and the joys, challenges, and sorrows I experienced when they were children are now experienced in different ways.

Does your life have this mix? Discomfort and stretching beyond what you feel you are able to bear? In everything, give thanks. Sometimes that's hard to do! I don't think we are called to be thankful for sin or destruction, but we can always give thanks for all He has done and given us in Christ Jesus, even amidst the challenges of life. This redirects our focus to Who He is instead of what we are going through.

At times this is with thankful tears, reminding ourselves He is in control, praying for grace, trusting in Him in the pain, and clinging to the truth that He is working out His plans for us. In the joys we can thank Him with singing, remembering His goodness and grace.

Whatever today holds, remember the One who holds it and give thanks.

Delight in Him

Psalm 1:1-39 (NKJV)
"Blessed is the man who walks not in the counsel of the ungodly,
nor stands in the path of sinners, nor sits in the seat of scornful.
But his delight is in the law of the Lord, and in His law he meditates day and night.
He shall be like a tree planted by the rivers of water,
That brings forth its fruit in its season,
Whose leaf also shall not wither, and whatever he does shall prosper."

"It's a good morning, wake up to a brand-new day!" I used to sing these lyrics by Christian music artist Mandisa to wake up my kids. For monotonous days that feel like the movie Groundhog Day, it's good to remember that God has made each day and we can rejoice in that.

I remember a time when I sat at the bedside of a man I cared for as a nurse. I had the opportunity to read Scripture to him. As I look back, I see how he made the first Psalm part of the fabric of his life. As The Moody Bible commentary by the Faculty of Moody Bible Institute describes the first two verses of this Scripture passage, he made it a "habit of walking with the Lord through His Word."

As I read Psalm 1 out loud, I watched this gentleman's lips recite the entire Psalm. It seemed to give him a calm steadiness and peace as he said it, even though his days on this earth were coming to an end. Did he want it read for his benefit or mine?

I don't remember much else about this gentleman or this visit, but I do recall that he seemed to delight in the law of the Lord and meditate on it. In doing this, it seemed to carry him through even his last days with a peace that passed all understanding. He appeared to have planted himself by rivers of living water and his leaves did not wither, even as his physical body had declined.

It is always such a blessing to remind myself of this special gift of the time this man spent with me. May you be blessed, as well, and make a "habit of walking with the Lord through His Word," so you may be planted by rivers of water and bring forth fruit in season.

Delight yourself in Him today.

El Shaddai

Isaiah 50:10 (NKJV)
"Who among you fears the Lord?
Who obeys the voice of His Servant?
Who walks in darkness
And has no light?
Let him trust in the name of the Lord
And rely upon his God."

Names can say a lot about a person. Their origins, meanings, and implications can remind you of why you may or may not enjoy a certain name.

I think my love for God's names originally came from my dad. Before he passed away more than 20 years ago, he had been writing a calendar with the names of God and corresponding Scriptures that gave regular reminders of Who God has revealed Himself to be in His Word.

I was able to finish this calendar many years after he went home to be with Jesus. This not only helped me process my grief, but also brought me closer to the Lord. In my study of His names since then, I have grown to love Him more.

During a number of rather painful medical procedures, the song "El Shaddai" by Michael Card was a comfort. I would sing this song to myself, and it brought me comfort and strength to endure the suffering. There are seasons of life when it's a lifeline to remember that He is El Shaddai, which is Hebrew for "God Almighty." He is able to do all things and sustain me through all things. He has been faithful before, and He will be faithful again.

Remembering God's name and worshiping Him for who He is strengthens my heart. Do any of the names of God have significance for you?

- El Shaddai — God Almighty, the God of Heaven
- Adonai — Lord, Master
- El Elyon — God Most High
- El Kanna — Consuming Fire, Jealous God
- El Roi — The God who sees me
- Yahweh Rophe — The Lord who heals

And these are just some of His glorious names! He is El Shaddai!

In Isaiah 50:10, the writer reminds us to trust in the name of the Lord and rely on our God in times of darkness or difficulties. Sometimes all we can do is cry out and say His name: Jesus, Jehovah is salvation. That's all we need to do, for He will fulfill all He has promised us.

He is El Shaddai!

Learning Contentment

Philippians 4:11-13 (NKJV)
"Not that I speak in regard to need, for I have learned in whatever state I am, to be content:
I know how to be abased, and I know how to abound.
Everywhere and in all things, I have learned both to be full and to be hungry,
both to abound and to suffer need.
I can do all things through Christ who strengthens me."

Stay at home restrictions, I'm done with you! I'm ready to resume "normal" life. I find it hard to be content as this season seems to be never ending.

I was reminded of this Philippians passage yesterday on a stress-relieving bike ride. As I was going up a hill, it came to mind that "I can do all things through Christ who strengthens me." As I repeated that over and over again in my mind, pretty soon I was up the hill.

Some hills in this life are steeper and longer than others, and right now I seem to be pedaling up a steep one. I'm weary and ready to be on the downhill slope. How do we learn, as the Apostle Paul wrote, to be content in whatever state we find ourselves in?

To put this passage in context, Paul was writing it from jail. He discovered that his contentment wasn't in his physical circumstances, but in the presence and sufficiency of Christ. Did he know isolation? Did he experience the need to see those he loved? Did he know feelings of frustration? What he found, and what we can find, is that through Christ's strength we can experience victory, regardless of our earthly circumstances.

A definition of contentment by Bill Gothard states, "Contentment is realizing that God has already provided everything we need for our present happiness." I used this quote in a DIY wall hanging with printer paper and an old picture frame, during a time in my life that required frugality. It served as a good reminder to look to God and thank Him for His provision.

Sometimes it frustrated me as I felt the pressures of life, and other times it brought me peace to remember that God is good and provides what I need to get through each season. It didn't magically make my needs go away, but I was able to turn my focus on Him and be content while continuing to seek Him for what I needed. How often we need this reminder when our attitudes need some help adjusting!

May you find the sweetness of being content in all things by God's sufficient grace.

Tender Mercies

Psalm 51:1-2, 10-12 (NKJV)
"Have mercy upon me, O God,
According to Your lovingkindness;
According to the multitude of Your tender mercies,
Blot out my transgressions.
Wash me thoroughly from my iniquity,
And cleanse me from my sin.
Create in me a clean heart, O God,
And renew a steadfast spirit within me.
Do not cast me away from Your presence,
And do not take Your Holy Spirit from me.
Restore to me the joy of Your salvation,
And uphold me by Your generous Spirit."

The sun is up, and its warmth encourages my heart to be thankful for another day. There is a song called "Create in Me a Clean Heart" that gives music to Psalm 51, and it's been running nonstop through my mind this morning. It's a cry out to the Lord for renewal, for cleansing, and for His tender mercies in the life of David after his sin with Bathsheba. Some days it can be our cry, too. I find it a beautiful prayer to God that is useful in different seasons of life.

In this chapter of the Psalms, David reminds himself that God is full of lovingkindness and has a multitude of tender mercies. Dwell on that picture for just a moment. What comes to mind? A soft warm summer breeze on the shores of the ocean of His love? A warm smile and hug from a loved one that cares for you unconditionally even when you've blown it?

God is merciful, and when David asks for forgiveness, he doesn't just stop there. He goes on to ask the Lord to create in Him a clean heart, renew a steadfast spirit, restore the joy of salvation, and uphold Him by

His Spirit. This is beautiful humility: To cry out to God in great need and recognize that He can blot out transgressions, cleanse, create, renew, restore, and uphold life. How great is our God!

Are you in need of His lovingkindness and tender mercies today? Do you long for a clean heart, for a steadfast spirit in Him, a return to joy of salvation, or an upholding of His Spirit today? Meditate on God's mercy and follow David's example to cry out to Him. In your need, God certainly will answer!

May you be enfolded by His tender mercies today.

He Knows

Job 23:10a (ESV)
"But He knows the way that I take ..."

As a parent, have you ever wanted to have constant GPS on your children's location? Have you, as a daughter or son, ever had a parent ask you to check in and want to know what you are doing?

It's comforting to know the status of your children and loved ones. I've been that parent that wants to know where my girls are. Let's be honest, sometimes I just want to check in on them! I love them and I want them to make right choices and be safe, healthy, and loved.

Our good Father knows the way we take. He has our location pinned permanently in His eternal, perfect GPS that is not subject to the limits of technology or human frailty. Doesn't it feel safe to know that Someone cares enough to always know where we are? This thought not only brings a smile to my face but a gentle comfort to my heart.

When things are difficult, painful, sorrowful, or unknown, it's such a sweet blessing to know God knows the way I take, understands where I am, and guides me with perfect wisdom as I trust and wait for His direction.

Are you thankful you're on God's radar? Is the location of your life one that you want Him to know? The sweetest grace is that even when our "locations" don't measure up to His perfection, He loves us anyway. That is why He sent His Son! He saw our path to destruction and went out on a rescue mission to save us. We can say to others as the Samaritan woman did in John 4:29, "Come, see a Man who told me all things that I ever did. Could this be the Christ?"

May you find comfort in knowing He knows.

Receive Him

John 1:11 (ESV)
"He came to His own and His own people did not receive Him."

There once was a story about a pastor that dressed in rags and sat in the front of his church. Many of his congregants did not want to shake his hand or receive him because of the way he was dressed, and they seemed to give preference to others because that seemed more "fitting." He later walked up to the podium to give that Sunday's sermon! I wonder how his congregation felt when they saw the man they had rejected stand up to preach.

The pastor's warning to his church was to be wary of showing favoritism. James 2:5 (NASB) asks, "Did God not choose the poor of this world to be rich in faith and heirs of the kingdom?" We are to give God alone the honor and glory He is due. He has called us to love our neighbor as ourselves, not show favor based on status or appearance.

When Jesus came to His people, the Jews, they did not receive Him as the Messiah. They knew much about Him, studied the Scriptures, worshiped in the temple, followed the commandments, passed down His stories from generation to generation, and yet when He stood right in front of them, they did not receive Him. Was it because He wasn't what they expected? Did He not look like the King they had pictured? Did they envision some other way for Him to come, rather than being born in a stable, riding on a donkey, or eating with sinners?

How often do we not receive Jesus in other areas of life when He may be right in front of us? How can we receive Him today in the gifts that He gives, whether it is dressed in a frustrating circumstance, a puppy with worms, or a child who is sick and keeps the washer running? How about a child with a strong independent will whose actions may reveal the limits of your patience, stay-at-home orders that seem never-ending, or changes in life that seem unfair? I'm challenged to look at His gifts with new eyes and receive what He has in each one.

Receive Him and His gifts today!

If the Lord Wills

James 4:13-15 (ESV)
"Come now, you who say, 'Today or tomorrow we will go into such and such
a town and spend a year there and trade and make a profit'—
yet you do not know what tomorrow will bring.
What is your life? For you are a mist that appears for a little time and then vanishes.
Instead, you ought to say, 'If the Lord wills, we will live and do this or that.'"

If anything, the days of COVID-19 have taught me how true this portion of Scripture is: "You do not know what tomorrow will bring." When I was on a hike at a retreat in February, the thought would have never crossed my mind that in one month's time I would be quarantined, working from home, my girls would be homeschooling, and life as I knew it would be shut down.

Have you ever been blindsided by your circumstances? The comforting part of today's Scripture is that God is sovereign. He knows the beginning, the end, and everything in between.

"With the Lord a day is like a thousand years, and a thousand years are like a day" (2 Peter 3:8 ESV). This Scripture reminds us that life is brief, "a mist that appears for a little time and then vanishes" (James 4:14 ESV). We would be wise to remember not only the brevity of this life, but also that we do not know what tomorrow will bring. As we make our plans, it would benefit us to acknowledge the Lord in all our ways and say, "Lord, if it be Your will."

During these days of the pandemic, I haven't wanted to make many plans. I don't have control over the opening of the country, and all my plans to move forward seem to hinge on things I can't control. Isn't this the reality, though? Don't our plans ultimately hinge on God, rather than us? I need to recognize daily that He is God, and I am not.

If the Lord wills, we will.

Be Still and Know

Psalm 46:10 (ESV)
"Be still and know that I am God; I will be exalted among the nations; I will be exalted in the earth!"

Are you feeling a little restless? During this COVID-19 stay-at-home order, I certainly am! This "new normal" is getting old for many, myself included.

Keith and Kristyn Getty wrote a beautiful hymn called "Still My Soul, Be Still." I would encourage you to listen to this song and allow the Lord to speak stillness and peace to your soul. Here is a line of the lyrics for you to ponder: "Lord of peace, renew a steadfast spirit within me to rest in You alone."

Have you ever seen a lake when there is no wind, and the top is like a sheet of glass? The sun reflects off of it like a glorious, beautifully framed picture. It reminds me of when the disciples were on the boat in the middle of the Sea of Galilee, and a storm arose when Jesus was sleeping in the boat (on a pillow, might I add!). As Mark records in his gospel, Jesus awoke at the pleading of His disciples and "rebuked the wind, and said to the sea, 'Peace be still!' And the wind ceased and there was a great calm" (Mark 4:35-41 ESV). If the winds and sea obey Him, He can certainly calm the restless storm within me.

Be still and know, my friend, that Jesus is Lord.

Rest in Him

Matthew 11:28-30 (ESV)
"Come to Me, all who labor and are heavy laden, and I will give you rest.
Take My yoke upon you, and learn from Me,
for I am gentle and lowly in heart, and you will find rest for your
souls. For My yoke is easy, and My burden is light."

In a recent conversation with a friend, we talked about the difficulty of getting into a rhythm with the changing schedule of this pandemic season. I was reminded of this passage in Matthew, and how The Message paraphrases verse 29 as "Learn the unforced rhythms of grace."

Isn't that a beautiful picture? Think of an experienced musician who plays an instrument with such smooth ability that it seems effortless. They weave together sound and rhythm to make a song that brings such beauty and such delight.

It's been challenging for me to find a new "rhythm" in these days that have seemed to take on a minor key. Do our hearts need His tuning?

Jesus tells us where to go when we feel such dissonance: "Come to Me." May He teach us all the rhythms of His grace and may our hearts forever sing His song. To Him be the glory, for He is gentle and lowly in heart, and we will find rest for our souls only in Him.

Find rest in the rhythms of His grace.

Grace Sufficient

2 Corinthians 12:9 (ESV)
"But He said to me, 'My grace is sufficient for you, for My power is made perfect in weakness.'"

I was recently reminded of my all-time favorite hymn, Amazing Grace, when I saw a video of an elderly man standing outside his wife's care facilities room window. She had Alzheimer's disease, and even though they were separated because of coronavirus restrictions, they sang Amazing Grace through the window to each other as she lay in bed.

This beautiful example of enduring love moved me to tears, not only because of this man's love for his bride, but also because of her ability, even with Alzheimer's, to sing along with her husband.

This song, because of its truths and reminders of His sufficient grace, has helped my family through some very difficult times, and I have often sung this to my girls through the years. May the Truth of His words in today's passage soothe and comfort your heart as we are reminded of the Lord's Amazing Grace, lavished on us daily.

His grace is sufficient!

Nothing Can Separate

Romans 8:35-39 (NKJV)
"Who shall separate us from the love of Christ? Shall tribulation, or distress, or persecution, or famine, or nakedness, or peril, or sword? As it is written: 'For Your sake we are killed all day long; We are accounted as sheep for the slaughter.' Yet in all these things we are more than conquerors through Him who loved us. For I am persuaded that neither death nor life, nor angels nor principalities nor powers, nor things present nor things to come, nor height nor depth, nor any other created thing, shall be able to separate us from the love of God which is in Christ Jesus our Lord."

Reminders of social distancing surround us right now. In every store there are marks on the ground, showing how far to stand from your neighbor. When I was in Target the other day, standing in the checkout line on a socially distanced red dot, the little boy in front of me stood with his feet exactly in the middle of the dot, his feet small enough to fit inside the circumference. His sweet innocence and childlike playfulness with the dots made my heart smile. It reminded me of fun interactive games, like Twister or Hullabaloo, that I used to play with my girls when their feet were little, too.

I was thankful for another beautiful sight while driving this morning. Two bald eagles were sitting next to each other in a very large dirt field, separate yet close together, in the cool of the morning air. It's good to take time to look around and remember the special blessings of each day.

My current reality includes mandatory mask wearing, 6 feet of distance between each person, and no large group gatherings. There is a lot of separateness going on right now. Humans are relational beings, and it's hard not to hug loved ones, shake hands, or use the power of touch to encourage others.

It's such a profound truth to remember in days of forced separateness or trials that nothing has any weight or ability to separate us from the amazing, powerful love of Christ. Through knowing God, believing His Word, and walking by faith, we are more than conquerors! He overcomes every adversary and adversity by the power of His name. He wins! Hallelujah!

As we seek and lean into Him, we, too, can say, 'In all these things we are more than conquerors through Him who loved us." This passage then states, "For I am persuaded ..." How are we persuaded of something? When we are persuaded, it means to come to know something as true. Are you persuaded that nothing shall be able to separate you from His love?

If you are not persuaded of this yet, I would encourage you to dig deep into the Bible, seek His face, look at the truth presented in Scripture, ask questions, seek godly counsel, talk to friends who have come to know His love, ask God Himself to reveal His love to you, and remember His daily faithfulness.

Nothing can separate us from the love of God!

Pray

Mark 1:35 (ESV)
"And rising very early in the morning, while it was still dark, he departed
and went out to a desolate place, and there he prayed."

We are experiencing separateness more now than we did before the pandemic. Feeling isolated can leave us with a negative view of being away from others. Yet, at times, separation is good, isn't it?

In today's passage from Mark, we see our Lord departing early in the morning and going to a desolate place to pray. Jesus' habit of seeking alone time with His Father is repeated many times throughout the gospel accounts. If Jesus was perfect, and still needed to depart many times in His earthly life to pray, we should follow His example all the more! Paul exhorts us, "Do not be anxious about anything, but in everything, by prayer and supplication, with thanksgiving, let your requests be made known to God" (Philippians 4:6 ESV).

Do you have daily requests that you bring to God? I certainly do! What an awesome thought that we can bring our requests to the Creator and King of the universe. Not only can we bring them to Him, He hears us!

Prayer is also an interaction between us and God as part of our relationship with our Heavenly Father. First Peter 3:12a (NKJV) states, "For the eyes of the Lord are on the righteous, and His ears are open to their prayers." In all the world, with all the people, God can hear our individual prayers. It's awe-inspiring, isn't it?

Sometimes my prayers are more requests than thanksgiving. Sometimes I'm filled with adoration and praise for Who He is and all He has done. Sometimes it's a cry for mercy and cleansing repentance, and sometimes it's silence. In some circumstances and seasons of this life, there are no words to bring to Him, just tears. He hears every heartfelt cry, every frustration, every need, every joy, every thought, and as He sees fit, He answers. Not in our time, not in our way, but in His perfect wisdom and goodness.

Take time to pray.

Thirsty for Him

Psalm 42:1-2 (NKJV)
"As the deer pants for the water brooks,
So pants my soul for You, O God.
My soul thirsts for God, for the living God.
When shall I come and appear before God?"

This is one of those Psalms that speaks to our needs. I have always loved word pictures from creation and think of them often. There is a song that was inspired by this Scripture that is such a beautiful heart cry to our Lord:

"As the deer panteth for the water
so my soul longeth after Thee.
You alone are my heart's desire
and I long to worship Thee."
("As the Deer," Martin Nystrom)

Even if you haven't seen a deer pant (I personally haven't), you've likely seen dogs pant for their water dishes in the heat of the day or after a long run. Once an animal reaches the water, they lap it up as if they've never had water before. Think of what it's like to have a cold cup of water on a hot summer day or after a strenuous workout. How refreshing is that water and how much do we appreciate it satisfying our thirst?

Our bodies need water to survive, and it's the same with our souls. Have you ever been in a spiritual drought where you're thirsty for God? Do you call out to Him as the Psalmist did?

In John's gospel, he writes about an exchange between a Samaritan woman and Jesus. Their conversation began with Jesus asking the woman for a drink, but it quickly turned to the thirst in the woman's heart. Jesus says in John 4:14 (NKJV), "... whoever drinks of the water that I shall give him will never thirst. But the water that I shall give him will become in him a fountain of water springing up into everlasting life."

If water on a parched tongue is refreshing relief, how much more reviving is Living Water washing over a thirsty soul!

May His water refresh your soul this day.

Edges of His Ways

Job 26:13-14 (NKJV)
"By His Spirit He adorned the heavens;
His hand pierced the fleeing serpent.
Indeed these are the mere edges of His ways,
And how small a whisper we hear of Him!
But the thunder of His power who can understand?"

"Mere edges of His ways." I love how Job uses this poetic language to help us grasp how much of God's power and majesty we do not know!

To be at the edge of something causes us to contemplate being at "a point near the beginning or end," according to Webster's Dictionary. But it also leaves us considering that there is much more left to be grasped. Have you considered how "His Spirit adorned the heavens" at the time of creation? How "His hand pierced the fleeing serpent" and brought all the constellations into existence with just a word? Yet these are the mere edges of His ways! Have you gazed upon the vast expanse of the sky filled with stars on a dark summer evening? Have you meditated on the vastness of each of the constellations known to the human eye? These are just the "mere edges of His ways."

How often we put God in a box without stopping to consider that He who made the heavens, and the earth is not able to be confined to the frailty of our own human imaginings!

Since we have only seen the mere edges of His ways, may we be reminded that He alone is worthy of our worship. May our hearts be comforted and know that He who wields all power (beyond our ability to comprehend!) also knows our days, the things we face and need, and loves us more than we can fathom.

Even on the mere edges, what a glorious sight to see!

His Glory, Our Valley

The Valley of Vision:
A Collection of Puritan Prayers and Devotions

"Lord, high and holy, meek and lowly,
Thou hast brought me to the valley of vision,
where I live in the depths but see Thee in the heights,
hemmed in by mountains of sin I behold Thy glory.
Let me learn by paradox that the way down is the way up,
that to be low is to be high…"

This excerpt from this beautiful prayer of the heart is a revealing picture of what it's like to live in God's economy. I would encourage you to take the time to read the rest of this prayer for your own personal study. There are glorious truths to learn in the valleys of life, even if it feels contrary to our human nature.

The "Valley of Vision" is referring to Jerusalem in Isaiah 22:1: "The burden against the Valley of Vision." A valley, by Webster's definition, is a "low point or condition" or a "depression of the earth's surface, usually between ranges of hills or mountains." Much of our lives are lived in the valley, and that is where we learn and grow the most. Those mountaintop experiences, albeit glorious and delightful, are meant for insight, refreshment, and strength, before going into the valley once again.

In the prayer above, the writer speaks of the chasm between sin and a holy God and the hope found in God. Contemplate the paradoxes noted above and in the remaining parts of this prayer. Consider how much more blessed it is to give than receive. How His joy is found in our sorrow. How His grace is found in our depths of sin, His riches in our poverty of spirit, and how His glory is seen in our valleys.

I'm reminded of these portions of Scripture from Jesus' Sermon on the Mount in Matthew 5:3-12 (NKJV): "Blessed are the poor in spirit, for theirs is the kingdom of heaven. Blessed are those who mourn, for they shall be comforted. Blessed are the meek, for they shall inherit the earth." Consider that Jesus taught this while He was up on a mountain. Sit on the mountain with Jesus, hear His words, and remember to see His glory in your valley by the light of His amazing grace.

May you see His glory in your valley.

Patience at Work

James 1:2-4 (NKJV)
"My brethren, count it all joy when you fall into various trials,
knowing that the testing of your faith produces patience.
But let patience have its perfect work,
that you may be perfect and complete, lacking nothing."

Patience, according to Vines dictionary, is "an abiding under" or "endurance." Patience, as seen here in James, is the result of the testing of our faith. There have been many seasons in my life when joy and trials go together about as well as oil and water. But as the Lord continues to work in my life, I can now look back and see the benefits of these trials and find the joy of growth toward spiritual maturity.

I remember a song that I used to sing with my kids about patience. It's a cute little jingle sung by Herbert the Snail called "The Fruit of the Spirit: Patience", by Candle. This jingle serves as a reminder to wait in the moment that feels too long:

"Have patience, have patience.
Don't be in such a hurry.
When you get impatient, you only start to worry.
Remember, remember that God is patient, too.
And think of all the times when others have to wait for you."

Patience is a gracious reminder of God's longsuffering nature toward us and our need for endurance in this life. Consider a marathon runner. They don't just go straight to the marathon from the couch. It's the stretching, the little runs, strength training, and longer runs throughout the training period that build the endurance and strength for the race.

God allows us to experience different trials with the ultimate goal of training, endurance, and spiritual maturity, complete and lacking nothing. His timing is perfect, and He is never late.

Let patience have its work in your heart!

Wholly Lean

Jude 24-25 (NKJV)
"Now to him who is able to keep you from stumbling
and to present you blameless before the presence of his glory with great joy,
to the only God, our Savior, through Jesus Christ our Lord,
be glory, majesty, dominion, and authority,
before all time and now and forever.
Amen."

I sit in silence before the Lord this morning as I meditate on this Scripture, enclosed in a card from a dear friend. I am painfully aware that the recent days have been discouraging, long, wearing, exhausting, frustrating, and confusing. But as I meditate on the praise and glory to God written at the end of Jude, I am encouraged and emboldened by the author's words. I hope they turn you toward the Lord to give Him praise and honor, too!

Consider His ability. Consider His omnipotence. Consider His divine transcendence. Consider His wisdom. Consider His infinitude. Can you even try to grasp it?

He is able, no matter what the future holds. He is all wise and all-knowing, regardless of life's confusion. He is all powerful, no matter what the difficulty. He is able to keep you, no matter what. Psalm 34:3 (ESV) says, "Oh, magnify the Lord with me, and let us exalt His name together!" He is able, even (and especially!) when we are not.

I'll close with these lyrics from "The Solid Rock," a hymn written by Edward Mote in the 1800s: "My hope is built on nothing less than Jesus' blood and righteousness. I dare not trust the sweetest frame, but wholly lean on Jesus' name."

To Him be the glory!

Dwell in Unity

Psalm 133:1 (ESV)
"Behold, how good and how pleasant
it is when brothers dwell in unity!"

The picture for May 2020 on my calendar is a church, with Psalm 133:1 written underneath. A timely reminder amidst pandemic days, times of unrest, differing opinions, misinformation, and division.

Behold! The psalmist wants to bring our attention to something above and beyond petty politics and earthly quarrels. Let's contemplate the goodness and pleasure of brethren who dwell together in unity.

What does the word "unity" bring to mind for you? Togetherness? Absence of strife? Harmony? Brotherly love? Don't these words sound pleasant to your ears? Isn't life more pleasant when we work to be at peace with one another? Oh, the goodness of dwelling in unity!

Achieving unity (and that ever-elusive dream of "world peace") can seem out of reach in this world full of strife, opposition, hatred, bitterness, and different personalities, but for those in the family of God, we have one Spirit that bonds us together. We are called to this!

in Ephesians 4:1-6 (NKJV), Paul encourages the church in Ephesus to "walk worthy of the calling with which you were called, with all lowliness and gentleness, with longsuffering, bearing with one another in love, endeavoring to keep the unity of the Spirit in the bond of peace. There is one body and one Spirit, just as you were called in one hope of your calling: one Lord, one faith, one baptism, one God and Father of all, who is above all, and through all, and in you all."

There is strength, goodness, and blessing in unity. How can you pursue it today?

His Blessing

Numbers 6:24-26 (NKJV)
"The Lord bless you and keep you;
the Lord make His face to shine upon you and be gracious to you;
the Lord lift up His countenance upon you and give you peace."

The Lord first gave these words to Moses for His people of Israel. He wanted to bless their obedience with His favor! What a glorious picture of the Lord's desire to bless obedience in His children!

The very first hospice patient I had the privilege of caring for would bless me with these words, "The Lord bless you and keep you," when I would leave for the day. What an expression of good he spoke over me!

Even to this day, I am still blessed by his words, inspired by Scripture, and say them often to loved ones. I pray that they would be blessed by the Lord and kept in His care, that His presence would be with them, that His grace and kindness would abound toward them, and that He would give them peace and overall wellbeing. What more do you need?

May the Lord bless you and keep you this day!

He is Greater

Psalm 77:16-20 (NKJV)
"The waters saw You, O God;
The waters saw You, they were afraid;
The depths also trembled.
The clouds poured out water;
The skies sent out a sound;
Your arrows also flashed about.
The voice of Your thunder was in the whirlwind;
The lightnings lit up the world;
The earth trembled and shook.
Your way was in the sea,
Your path in the great waters,
And Your footsteps were not known.
You led Your people like a flock
By the hand of Moses and Aaron."

It's helpful for me to remember the greatness and strength of our God. We live in troubling times, and where difficulties abound for many, we must remember who God is.

The psalmist recounts the deliverance of the people through the Red Sea: "When the waters saw You, they were afraid; The depths also trembled." This Psalm was written from the perspective of depression, but by verse 10, the writer refocuses his mind on God and turns to praise, remembering His faithfulness and blessings. We could all benefit from learning this cycle that the Psalmist models so often: lament, refocus, remember, and praise.

I was driving down the road one summer day, windows down, and a very large bug landed on my shoulder. I do not consider myself a bug person, so immediately my insides cringed, and I had the overwhelming desire to be as far away from the bug as possible! But then this thought entered my mind: "I am bigger than the bug." What a profound (and totally obvious) thought! This helped me take a breath and get rid of the bug in a very sensible manner out my window.

I hope my plight brings a smile and maybe a little laughter to your day. I realize this may be an oversimplified word picture, but hopefully you'll see the parallel with what we're dealing with right now. God is bigger than the COVID-19 "bug" or any other bug that disrupts our lives. Psalm 77:19 (ESV), "Your way was through the sea, your path through the great waters, and yet your footsteps were unseen." How mysterious and great is our God!

Isn't it wonderful to know that God is bigger than whatever problem we face that may seem to overwhelm, drown, or scare us? "Who has held the oceans in His hands? Who has numbered every grain of sand? Kings and nations tremble at His voice! All creation rises to rejoice! Behold our King! Nothing can compare! Come let us adore Him!" ("Behold Our God," Sovereign Grace Music)

How great is our God!

Draw Nearer

James 4:8a (NKJV)
"Draw near to God, and he will draw near to you."

The hymn "Nearer My God to Thee" reminds me of this verse in James. I discovered it was written in the 1800s by Sarah Flower, after hearing a sermon on Genesis 28:11-19. In the passage, God reveals Himself to Jacob in a dream, reminding him of His promise to Jacob's grandfather, Abraham. When Jacob awoke, he declared, "Surely the Lord is in this place, and I did not know it" Genesis 28:16b (NKJV).

Whenever I reflect on this verse, I've often prayed, "Lord, make me aware of Your presence." As the distractions and pressures of the day unfold, I am reminded of the need to draw near to Him and am reassured by His promise that He will draw near to me. This comforting promise by a truthful God brings peace and joy to my heart. He is Emmanuel, "God with us."

Let us draw near, pursue a relationship with Him with confidence, and trust that He will draw near to us. Then we can declare as Jacob did, "Surely the Lord is in this place!"

Draw near.

He for Me

1 John 4:9-10 (NKJV)
"In this the love of God was manifested toward us,
that God has sent His only begotten Son into the world,
that we might live through Him.
In this is love, not that we loved God,
but that He loved us
and sent His Son to be the propitiation for our sins."

One evening during dinner, I asked my sweet husband for "tea for two." As he poured, he recited an old song with a twinkle in his eye: "Tea for two, me for you, and you for me." His loving words made my heart smile.

Me for you. Such generosity in those words. Isn't that what Jesus came to do? He for me, to give Himself a ransom for many. Charles Wesley sums up his amazement in these words in his song, "And Can It Be?" "Amazing love! How can it be? That Thou, my God, shouldst die for me?"

Sit and bask in His amazing love today, contemplate His goodness, and have some "teatime" with Him. Let Him pour His love into your soul, remembering what He gave "that we might live through Him."

He for you, He for me.

Commit Your Way

Psalm 37:5 (ESV)
"Commit your way to the Lord;
trust in Him, and He will act."

In a past journal entry, I wrote, "Our actions will show where our loyalty lies." I'm not sure where that came from that day, but ponder this for a moment: What did your actions of yesterday say about your loyalties?

Is your life all about you? Your needs, wants, and desires?

Is it about others? Serving, loving, caring, and giving?

Is it all about Jesus? His will, His glory, and His purposes?

This mental exercise is a good place for self-evaluation. Loyalty can be such an honorable trait, but when our loyalties reside in the wrong place, our actions will show it.

2 Timothy 2:13 (ESV) shows us that God is the ultimate picture of loyalty. "If we are faithless, He remains faithful." How gracious and loving is our God. His actions will always declare His heart toward those who believe. And that, my friend, should bring great joy and peace to our hearts.

Let us commit our ways to the Lord today.

The Same Yesterday and Today

Hebrews 13:8 (KJV)
"Jesus Christ is the same yesterday, and today, and forever."

How comforting are the words of God when I search His Word first in the morning for His daily grace. In times of much uncertainty, we can be certain of this: He is the same yesterday, today and forever!

Ultimately, God is in control of all things, and we can only control how we choose to respond to the challenges we face. Even with this truth in mind, we can certainly struggle with anxiety in uncertain times. We must be diligent to focus our hearts on the One who never changes and rules overall.

During this pandemic crisis, we are tangibly feeling the changes and control of our governing authorities. The plans and goals we'd set, which once seemed achievable, now seem unsettled and uncertain.

As anxieties within your heart may rise, let His comfort enfold you. No purpose of His can be withheld (Job 4:2 NKJV), and He uses all things to work together for the good of those who love Him and are called according to His purpose (Romans 8:28 NKJV). Our plans and goals may change, but when we look to His ultimate purpose to conform us to the image of His Son, we find that He will use trials and difficulty to grow us into image-bearers of His Son.

Find comfort in Him Who never changes!

Lean Into Hope

Lamentations 3:21-22 (KJV)
"This I recall to my mind, therefore I have hope. It is of the Lord's mercies
that we are not consumed, because his compassions fail not."

When I feel tired, ready to give up, this I recall to my mind: Therefore, I have hope, because His compassions fail not. Consider what not failing looks like. We are all too familiar with failing in our broken sinful nature, but what hope to serve the One whose compassions never fail!

Lean into His possibility in your impossible circumstances, lean into His never-ending lovingkindness in your end, lean into His unfailing compassions in your suffering, lean into His new daily mercies in the mundane aspects of life, and thus be renewed every day for great is His faithfulness. He is God and there is no one like Him.

Lean in and have hope!

Waiting and Watching

Psalm 130:3-6 (KJV)
"If thou, Lord, shouldest mark iniquities, O Lord, who shall stand? But there is forgiveness with Thee, that Thou mayest be feared. I wait for the Lord, my soul doth wait, and in His word do I hope. My soul waiteth for the Lord more than they that watch for the morning: I say, more than they that watch for the morning."

Have you ever watched the morning roll in? Held a steaming cup of coffee and watched the sun peek over the mountaintops and the sky's darkness gradually lift to shine the light of day? For its timing, each day is known to all. You can just check your weather app and the sunrise time is there. As I consider this Scripture passage, I am reminded yet again of His faithfulness. The Creator and sustainer of our lives and of this world, who calls the sun to rise as He wills, is never late. He is always on time and faithful in His ways. As we wait expectantly for the morning sun to rise, let us wait with glorious anticipation on the Lord and always hope in His unfailing Word!

Wait and watch for the Lord today!

Follow Me

Matthew 4:19a (HCSB)
"'Follow Me,' He told them."

I consider this verse in light of our social media culture where we count followers and choose to follow people with the click of a button. How much do we truly consider this choice in that realm? We must be careful and wise about who we follow in this life. Consider that, when we follow someone, we must trust where they may take us. Do they lead us closer to Jesus or closer to the world?

I'm thankful that when Jesus commands us to follow Him, He knows where He is going, and it is always for our good and His glory. He won't lead us astray!

We must also, in light of this, be mindful of who may be following us. Ensuring that we lead others to Christ in the way we talk, act, and love in life. How could we do this apart from Him? We cannot. In order to lead well those that may follow us, we must follow closely to the One who is the way.

Follow Him!

Ebb and Flow

Isaiah 33:6a (NASB)
"And He will be the stability of your times."

I grew up near the ocean and always loved the times when the tide went out. The shells are easily seen, the sand is wet and smushes between your toes, and the sand crabs are busy burrowing under the sand, their tiny holes seen for a brief moment. And when the tides roll in, it's quite fun to watch chairs moving away from the incoming waters, the increasing waves, and the sandcastles melting away. How these ebbs and flows all come with their own set of beauties!

Life, too, ebbs and flows with the seasons God allows in our lives. Through the past year, the ebb of change from the things we once knew has seemed much longer and to a greater extent than I've known before. The beautiful truth is God doesn't ebb and flow with the season, the tides, or the culture. He truly is the stability of our times and this is where we can stand and keep ourselves from being washed away in the ebbs and flows of life.

Hold on to His stability today!

Decrease

John 3:30 (NASB)
"He must increase, but I must decrease."

"Let it go." What comes to mind when you read those words? Maybe a popular children's movie song or a platitude? Either way, the phrase can seem much easier and lighter than the actual weight of the action. Letting go is certainly not easy at times. Pride and selfishness get in the way as I choose to hold onto things that God wants me to hand to Him. It's usually a painful process, at times with blood, sweat and tears. But with His help, I can get myself out of the way so that God is in His rightful place on the throne of my heart.

What areas do you need to decrease in so that He can increase? Do you want your desires more than God's will?

With all the changes this pandemic has brought to us, we have felt the pain of losing control by having to let go of our plans and desires of the present. It has been painful and challenging, to say the least. However, may this be an opportunity to remind us that, with Jesus, anything we let go of or lose to Him is not lost in Christ. We always gain more of Him than we could ever lose.

May His increase be your gain.

Steadfast on Him

Isaiah 26:3 (NKJV)
"You will keep him in perfect peace,
Whose mind is stayed on You,
Because he trusts in You."

In this last devotional, I thought it fitting to send you off with encouragement to continue to fix your mind and trust on Him, no matter what life brings. He is faithful, He is Lord of all, and He gives peace this world severely lacks — His perfect peace.

Jesus spoke to His disciples more than once about peace before returning to His Father in Heaven. "Peace I leave with you, My peace I give to you; not as the world gives do I give to you. Let not your heart be troubled, neither let it be afraid" (John 14:27 ESV).

In John 16:33 (NKJV), He says, "These things I have spoken to you, that in Me you may have peace. In the world you will have tribulation; but be of good cheer, I have overcome the world."

Jesus didn't promise His gift of peace in trouble-free days. He promised it amidst the trouble of the world because He has overcome it all!

May He continue to lead you beside still waters as you trust in Him.

Closing Thoughts

As I started on this publishing journey, there were so many doubts and thoughts that entered my mind. Will anyone read this? Will anyone know my heart is to encourage theirs? Will others know that my desire is to comfort and strengthen them with His truth in this trial we all face? I'm not sure I have any of these answers. However, if one life is encouraged and drawn closer to God, it has all been worth it.

Within 2 days of the time when I reached out to a publisher regarding this devotional, I was dramatically affected by COVID-19 when my older brother was placed in the ICU on a ventilator with the virus. It was heart-wrenching to walk through, compounded by the fact that just 3 years prior I had been in the same ICU saying goodbye to another brother who is now with Jesus.

By God's sweet mercy and grace, my brother, after 21 days in the ICU, began his recovery. The scenarios that plagued my mind during those days, the fear and pain that gripped my heart, are all very real. Having to wait from home as he sat in the hospital alone, only able to be placed on speaker or have a video call through the ICU glass to see his status is dreadful. Waiting on the calls of doctors and nurses daily, hoping for some good news or a change in the right direction only to be met with another setback or new challenge to his health is beyond words to describe. And yet remembering that day — oh that blessed day — when the phone call came, saying my brother was off the ventilator and waking up. The tears of joy and thanksgiving that flowed through my heart as I knelt to the ground in such gratitude are forever etched on my heart.

During those 21 days I prayed, I waited, I cried, I reached out for support, and I leaned into God's comfort and love. I remember one night while he was there, I was sitting on the phone at home while on speaker phone in his ICU room, saying a prayer and reading Scripture aloud to him. For a few moments I sat listening to the machines in silence, wondering what the future would hold.

It is almost like time stops when tragedies and trials strike. The days seem long and the nights longer. I don't know what the future holds in this life for any of us, but I am certain of this: The One who holds it will continue to give abounding grace and comfort for anything we face and will be with me every step of the way.

Grace and Peace to you,

Jennifer

Acknowledgments

To my dear husband, Preston. Thank you for always spurring me onward in this endeavor and for your love each and every day.

To my precious daughters, Abby & Addi. You mean the world to me and I am honored to be your mother. Thank you for shining so brightly for Jesus and for your regular encouraging words and affirmations to me. You both bring so much joy to my life and I am forever grateful to God for you. I love you always.

To my sweet Mom, who shared some of her editing skills for this book, encouraged me, loved me, and supported me through this journey. She is a special gift from the Lord. Thank you for pointing me to Him. Your perseverance through trials and never-give-up attitude through the hardships of life continue to strengthen my own resolve to press on. I love you so much.

To my dear friend, Amanda, who spent hours editing and reformatting these devotionals to make them book ready, I'm so grateful for how you have allowed God to use your gifts and talents to help make this possible. You are a true gem.

Bonus Content
Lessons From My Dad

Philippians 1:21 (NASB)
"For to me, to live is Christ, and to die is gain."

As I often have looked through my dad's devotional journals that I have kept from his life and walk with Jesus, it allows me to feel close to him and also gives me encouragement along the way. My father went to be with Jesus at the age of 50 after a short battle with cancer, when I was just 19 years old. I miss him often and have longed for his presence so many times in my life. With this unfulfilled longing, this side of heaven, it has drawn me to find fullness, wholeness, and healing in the Presence of my heavenly Father, and I am forever grateful.

May these small bits of wisdom I have gleaned from my dad's journals draw you to your Heavenly Father's everlasting arms.

- I must not demand an answer from God, instead seek God who gives the answer.
- Let the past sleep, as God is our rear guard.
- Living Sacrifice - Not giving up things for the sake of giving them up, but to be free for God's service.
- Arise and do the next thing. Never let the sense of failure corrupt your new action.
- Live looking to God through Jesus Christ.
- The point of asking Him is that you may get to know God better.
- Out of the wreck I rise every time.
- Do I turn to what God says or what I fear?
- I am certain of one thing about my life: How easy it is for me to be wrong.
- Don't fret, our circumstances are not too much for God.
- Yes, Lord.
- Nothing in my hand I bring, only to Jesus I cling.
- More of Christ.
- His timing, not mine.
- Remember Whose you are.

Do any of these thoughts resonate with you? Take time to meditate on them, journal Scriptures that come to mind, and ask God for what you need. Let Jesus speak to your heart through His Word.

In closing, here are a few prayer notes from my dad. May they encourage your hearts to love Him more.

- May I entrust to You, the very keeping of my soul. Father, we must go Your Way in Jesus' name.
- Lord Jesus, today lift our hearts as we lift them to Thee.
- Keep this little one as the apple of your eye, Lord Jesus.
- Father, we have believed in Your Son, we want Your will!
- May Your grace extend even here, thank you.

In Jesus' Name, Amen.

Printed in the United States
by Baker & Taylor Publisher Services